Good English

Boswell Taylor

Headway · Hodder & Stoughton

Notes for Parents and Teachers

The importance of English usage is stressed in the National Curriculum now introduced into schools. In the opening paragraph of the Introduction is the statement:

> Language is the means of learning throughout the school curriculum and throughout every key stage ... *It is essential* that opportunities are created to develop children's *learning through language, about language and as users of language*, in all curriculum areas.

This is a basic work book that reinforces the use of language. It is not a grammar book, but is entirely concerned with the use of the English language. Grammar is a system of language, and usage is the way that people use that system, which is the way that people use words.

The book is divided into three sections: 'Building a vocabulary', 'Using a vocabulary' and 'Choosing the correct word'. The final section is also about 'Choosing the interesting word'.

Each double page is concerned with a single aspect of the subject. Usually a rule is given, explained with examples, and exercises follow. Tests are provided at the end of each section, prefaced with *Now test yourself*. Answers to these tests are given at the end of the book. The final test has a rating chart so that the student can estimate his or her degree of success.

It is impossible within the limits of a 32-page book to cover the whole subject, and a work book cannot supply open-ended questions to stimulate the further development of the work. It is hoped, however, that the work will simplify and entice, and arouse within children a love of words and an appreciation of the English language.

A good up-to-date dictionary is an invaluable support. A further 'treasure house' (as its name, taken from the Greek, implies) is Roget's *Thesaurus*.

Contents

analogies, 22
antonyms, 14, 15
association, 23
classification, 18–21
collective nouns, 20, 21
dictionary work, 4, 5
gradation, 23
idioms, 25
prefixes, 8, 9

similes, 22
suffixes, 10, 11
synonyms, 16, 17
tests, 13, 24, 30
   answers, 31–2
vocabulary, 6–12
   correct, 25–7
   interesting, 28–9

Facts about English Usage

English is a living language. Every invention introduces new words into the language. The car gave a new meaning to *bonnet*. The computer has brought into common use a whole series of new words, such as *algorithm* and *software*. An increasing awareness of the dangers to our environment has given us *ozone layer* and the *greenhouse effect*. If people use a word it will be entered in dictionaries, and become a part of the English language. While new words are born, some words die because they are no longer used. Perhaps *frock* will die in this way.

This book is about words and how we use them. The first of three sections is about 'Building a vocabulary'. It tells how a vocabulary can grow. Many words are made up of parts – like the game of *Lego*. The basic part – the *root* – probably came from a language such as Latin or Greek. Then parts can be added to vary the meaning of the word. Port came from Latin and meant *carry*. Put *im-* in front of it and we have import (carried into the country). Add *ex-* and we have export (carried out of the country). What is described when we add *trans-*?

The second section is about 'Using a vocabulary'. In this section we learn how to make full use of the vocabulary we are acquiring. We learn about opposites and words that mean the same, and the part that each member of a family of words can play.

The third section is about 'Choosing the correct word'. Our language is so rich that there is usually a word to describe every shade of meaning we wish to express. One word can be used instead of many. In this section, too, we learn about interesting words. Some of these words resemble the sounds they describe. The Greeks called it *onomatopoeia* which means 'word-making'. Two onomatopoeic words are cuckoo and sizzle. When we know that, it all seems very much simpler. That is mainly the purpose of this book: to make an important study, that may seem daunting at first, simple to understand and fun to do.

Using the dictionary

A dictionary contains words with their meanings and other information about them. An up-to-date dictionary keeps pace with changes in English usage and provides guidelines for the correct use of the language. All the words in the English language are formed from the alphabet of 26 letters:

a b c d e f g h i j k l m n o p q r s t u v w x y z

For easy reference the entry words in the dictionary are usually arranged in alphabetical order. The first letter is the most important:

*a*nger   *c*osmos   *f*rizzle   *j*abber   *s*afari

Write these words in alphabetical order:

A 1 *l*emon   *t*alc   *h*obbit   *b*ingo   *r*iddle   *a*nkle   *s*pinnaker

ankle, bingo, hobbit, lemon, riddle, spinnaker, talc.

2 *t*hane   *g*ondolier   *m*otor   *v*anilla   *d*ungeon   *O*lympic

dungeon, gondolier, motor, Olympic, thane, vanilla

When the first letters are the same, the words are arranged according to the second letters:

*ad*dle   *Al*satian   *ar*cade   *as*tronaut   *au*tobiography

Write these words in alphabetical order:

B 1 *ba*seball   *be*tray   *by*e   *bi*llabong   *bu*oy

baseball, betray, billabong, buoy, bye

2 *mi*dget   *mu*ntjak   *M.T.*B.   *me*ridian   *ma*tador

matador, meridian, midget, M.T.B., muntjak

When the first two letters are the same, the words are arranged according to the third letters:

*fla*mingo   *Fle*mish   *fli*bbertigibbet   *flu*gelhorn

Write these words in alphabetical order:

C 1 poet   polony   point-blank   pommy   P.O.P.   Port Salut

poet, point-blank, polony, pommy, P.O.P., Port Salut

2 reference   relax   rennet   R.E.M.E.   regent   replica

reference, regent, relax, R.E.M.E., rennet, replica

A dictionary gives the definition (meaning) of words.

Write the dictionary definition for each of the following:

A 1 nimbo-stratus *low dark-grey layer of cloud*
  2 soothsayer *on who predicts events or developments*
  3 manifesto *qualifications of a person or group*
  4 strontium *soft silver-white metallic element*
  5 fumerole *smoke/fumes*

Answer the following questions using the dictionary definition in each case:

B 1 In which country is parliament known as the *Cortes*?
    The Cortes is the parliament of Spain

  2 What are the colours of a palomino?
    The colours of a palomino are golden or cream

  3 What does a spelunker explore for sport? — *exploring caves*

  4 What animal may carry a howdah on its back? — *litter*

Some words have more than one meaning. Each definition is given in the dictionary.

plumb: 1 ball of lead; 2 sound (sea) or measure with plummet; 3 work as a plumber.

Give an alternative meaning for each of the following:

C 1 fleece: Strip a person of money, property, etc.
    Fleece is the woolly covering of sheep or similar animals

  2 jeer: Scoff derisively at, deride. Gibe, taunt.
    To show contempt by derision or mockery

  3 rick: Stack of hay, corn, peas, etc.
    cover to protect from rain

  4 negus: Ruler of Ethiopia

Building a vocabulary – roots

A root is the part of the word that contains its basic meaning. Most roots in English come originally from Latin and Greek words. New words are often invented by combining roots:

    tele (far) + vis (sight) + ion (condition of) = television

Here is a list of important Latin roots:
    cent- (hundred)   fac- (make, do, act)   fall- (deceive, make mistakes)
    labor- (work)   nov- (new)

Write words from the dictionary which are derived from the following roots:

A 1 *cent-* Century.. Centenarian. Centipede
    2 *fac-*
    3 *fall-*
    4 *labor-*
    5 *nov-*

Here is a list of important Greek roots:
    aster- (star)   bibl- (book)   ge- (earth)
    phil- (friend)   oct- (eight)

Write words from the dictionary which are derived from the following roots:

B 1 *aster-*
    2 *bibl-*
    3 *ge-*
    4 *phil-*
    5 *oct-*

Write words from the dictionary which are derived from the following roots:

C 1 *aqua-*   (water)
    2 *audio-* (hear)
    3 *aequ-* (equal)
    4 *neur-*   (nerve, tendon)
    5 *top-*   (place)

Some roots come at the end of words: agog- (lead, bring) → demagogue synagogue

Here are lists of words with a common root. Use the dictionary to find the meaning of any word you do not know.

Write the common meaning of the root words in the following:

D 1 de*ject*, in*ject*, e*ject* .. throw

    2 big*amy*, mono*gamy*, amal*gam*, poly*gamy* ....

    3 *cede*, re*cede*, se*cede* ....

    4 ver*dict*, pre*dict*, e*dict* ....

    5 de*scribe*, *script*, manu*script* ....

Roots can come at the beginning, in the middle or at the end of a word: tract (draw) → tractor, attraction, detract

Underline the root word in the following and give its meaning:

E 1 <u>port</u>er, ex<u>port</u>, im<u>port</u>, trans<u>port</u>, <u>port</u>able . carry

    2 autograph, biography, graph, stenography ....

    3 diameter, metronome, symmetry, thermometer ....

    4 expel, propel, propeller, repel, impel ....

    5 pedal, pedestrian, quadruped, pedicure ....

Write words from the dictionary that are derived from the following roots:

F 1 *path-* (feeling) . pathetic . pathos . pathology

    2 *grand-* (great) ....

    3 *oct-* (eight) ....

    4 *tort-* (twist) ....

    5 *vol-* (wish) ....

G 1 *soph-* (wise) ....

    2 *scope-* (see) ....

    3 *zo-* (animal living) ....

    4 *typ-* (model, impression) ....

    5 *cosmo-* (universe) ....

Building a vocabulary – prefixes

A word may be built up or have its meaning changed by an addition at the beginning (prefix) or at the end (suffix).

Here is a list of important prefixes:
- ante- (before)   bi- (two)   re- (back)
- ex- (out of)   trans- (across)   contra- (against)

Write words from the dictionary which use the following prefixes:

A 1 *ante-* antechamber anteroom antedate
  2 *bi-* ....
  3 *re-* ....
  4 *ex-* ....
  5 *trans-* ....
  6 *contra-* ....

Write words from the dictionary which use the following prefixes:

B 1 *ab-*   (away, from) ....
  2 *ambi-*   (both) ....
  3 *anti-*   (against) ....
  4 *auto-*   (self) ....
  5 *bene-*   (good, well) ....
  6 *circum-* (round) ....

C 1 *hemi-*   (half) ....
  2 *inter-* (between) ....
  3 *mis-*   (wrong) ....
  4 *peri-*   (around) ....
  5 *poly-*   (many) ....
  6 *super-* (above, over) ....
  7 *tri-*   (three) ....
  8 *post-*   (after) ....
  9 *pre-*   (before) ....

A prefix can be added to give a word its opposite meaning. These prefixes are:

un- (not, without)   dis- (not)   in- (not)   im- (not)
il- (not)   ir- (not)   non- (not)   de- (undo)

Complete the following, adding a prefix to give the opposite meaning:

D 1 Susan is .... **ir**.regular in her attendance at school.

2 This letter is an ...... important document.

3 The twins were ...... polite to their uncle.

4 It is ...... legal to park the car on the pavement.

5 The express was a .... -stopping train.

6 The army must be ...... mobilized.

Some prefixes have matching opposites:

ex- (out of)   bene- (good)   pre- (before)   a- (on)
im- (in, into)   mal- (bad)   post- (after)   de- (down)

Rewrite the following to give the opposite meaning (note the pairs above):

E 1 The genii that appeared was *malevolent* in expression.

The genii that appeared was benevolent in expression.

2 The *imported* cars travelled in container ships.

....

3 The mansion was a *post-war* building.

....

4 We must *ascend* the stairs to get to the playroom.

....

Underline the prefix in the following, and write its meaning, using the dictionary:

F 1 <u>ab</u>normal, <u>ab</u>sent, <u>ab</u>duct . *away, from* ....

2 circumstance, circumnavigate, circumvent ....

3 extraordinary, extravagant, extramural ....

4 multiply, multitude, multi-millionaire ....

5 ambivalent, ambiguous, ambidexterous ....

6 ex-president, ex-footballer, ex-governor ....

Building a vocabulary – suffixes

The suffix is added to the end of a word.
The prefix usually changes the meaning of a word. The suffix changes its function rather than its meaning.
Some suffixes signify *state of*, *quality of*, *act of*.

    cowardice – the quality of a coward

Underline the suffix in the following words; and write it separately:

A 1 democracy, accuracy . - *acy* . . .   2 marriage, drainage . . . .

    3 repentance, utterance . . . .   4 operation, starvation . . . .

    5 freedom, kingdom . . . .   6 boyhood, falsehood . . . .

    7 avarice, cowardice . . . .   8 baptism, communism . . . .

    9 enjoyment, merriment . . . .   10 happiness, blindness . . . .

    11 friendship, hardship . . . .   12 security, modesty . . . .

Note that spellings sometimes have to be changed when the suffix is added.
Some suffixes signify a *person*, *one who does*.

    baker – one who bakes   equestrian – one who rides a horse

Underline the suffix in the following words, and write it separately:

B 1 dentist, typist . . -*ist* . . . .   2 labourer, banker . . . .

    3 hostess, stewardess . . . .   4 auctioneer, mountaineer . . . . . .

    5 employee, trainee . . . .   6 gangster, trickster . . . .

Add a suffix to the underlined words to signify a person (drop the *s*):

C 1 a person who hunts . *hunter* . .   2 a person who sells hats . . . .

    3 a woman who waits upon customers at a café . . . .

    4 a man who waits upon customers at a café . . . .

Change the following words to signify a female:

D 1 lion . . . .   2 count . . . .

    3 prince . . . .   4 god . . . .

Using suffixes

Here are some suffixes with their meanings:

-able, -ible	capable of being	-ant, -ent	one who
-el, -est, -ette	little	-ful	full of
-fy	to make, do	-icle, -sel	little
-less	without	-ory, -ary	a place for
-ous	full of	-ling	little
-oon, -on	large	-let	little

Complete the following definitions with one of the suffixes listed above:

E 1 A fact **ory**.. is a building in which things are manufactured.

2 A mor...... is a small piece, a mouthful.

3 A kitchen...... is a small kitchen in a flat.

4 A stud...... is a person who attends college.

5 To simpli...... is to make things easier to do or understand.

6 A ball...... is an airtight inflated envelope.

7 A port...... canoe is one that is easy to carry.

8 A pig...... is a young pig.

9 A fam...... person is celebrated for deeds of renown.

10 A guilt...... person is innocent of misdeeds.

11 A duck...... is a young duck.

12 A care...... person always tries to do well.

The suffix *-ery* is usually added to words of one syllable.

The suffix *-ry* is usually added to words of more than one syllable.

Add the suffix *-ery* or *-ry* to the following:

F 1 *goods or things*   green **ery**.........., drap **ery**..............

2 *employment*   dentist ...., cook ....

3 *place of work*   brew ...., bak ....

4 *home or abode*   rook.............., nunn ....

5 *conduct*   rival.............., fool ....

Building a vocabulary – substitutes for over-used words

'Awful' is used to describe various degrees or kinds of nastiness. Words that might be used to better effect are:

unpleasant   fearful   loathsome   appalling   silly

Complete the following sentences, using one of the words in the above list:

A 1 Derek made a . **silly**. . . . . mistake in his arithmetic test.

   2 We wondered what caused the . . . . smell in the kitchen.

   3 The wounded dragon sank into the . . . . slime.

   4 Three people were killed in the . . . . road accident.

   5 The . . . . ghost appeared once more in the haunted house.

'Got' is often used in a lazy way. Better substitutes could be:

got: gained, obtained   got to: arrived   got away: escaped   got up: arose

Complete the following, using the most appropriate word from the list:

B 1 The prisoner . **escaped**. . . . . . . from the jail.

   2 The traveller . . . . before the train left.

   3 Every morning Fiona . . . . at seven o'clock.

   4 Jonathan . . . . his safety first medal.

   5 He . . . . the groceries at the supermarket.

'Nice' has lost its original meaning which was 'elegant'. Substitutes are:

pretty   delicious   interesting   dainty   enjoyable

C 1 The children were happy watching the . **enjoyable**. . . . . . film.

   2 Deborah wore a . . . . dress for the party.

   3 The peaches were ripe and . . . .

   4 The book was . . . . and full of facts.

   5 The . . . . fairies danced on tip-toe round the tree.

Substitute   advance   enter   exit   forward   for the following phrases:

D 1 go forward . **advance**. . . . . . .   2 go up . . . .

   3 go away . . . .   4 go into . . . .

★Now test yourself on building a vocabulary

Arrange the following in alphabetical order:

A 1 monster   wampum   Kalmuck   autogiro   lumbago
   ....

  2 plump   plough   plasticine   plateau   plonk
   ....

  3 condor   concert   convent   concrete   condemn
   ....

  4 galipot   Dixie   gadzooks   sanctuary   dividend
   ....

Underline the root parts of the following:

B 1 liberty   infallible   October   import   navigate
  2 laboratory   tentacles   unity   repel   politics
  3 pedestrian   primitive   manual   fortify   rotund
  4 revoke   decimal   creature   aqueduct   revolve

Underline the root part of the following and give its meaning:

C 1 abstract, traction, protract ....
  2 pathos, sympathy, antipathy ....
  3 pedal, pedestrian, quadruped ....
  4 diameter, metronome, thermometer ....

Underline the prefix in the following and give its meaning:

D 1 predict, precede, prepare ....
  2 transpose, transfer, transport ....
  3 international, interrupt, intervene ....

Underline the suffix in the following and give its meaning:

E 1 thoughtful, thankful, regretful ....
  2 applicant, servant, assistant ....
  3 lioness, waitress, princess ....

13

Antonyms or words opposite in meaning

An antonym is a word that is opposite in meaning to a given word. Antonyms can be formed in four ways.

1 By adding one of the following prefixes (see page 9):
   un-   dis-   in-   im-   (most common)
   il-   (less common)

Add prefixes to give words opposite in meaning to the following:

A 1 *dis*..advantage   2 ......approve   3 ......pleasure
    4 ......happy   5 ......fair   6 ......wise
    7 ......audible   8 ......complete   9 ......human
    10 ......polite   11 ......possible   12 ......mortal
    13 ......legal   14 ......legible   15 ......literate

2 By changing one of the following prefixes:
   ab- ↔ pre-   em- ↔ im-   a- ↔ de-   en- ↔ dis-
   in- ↔ ex-   min- ↔ max-   pro- ↔ anti-   in- ↔ de-

Use one of the above listed prefixes to give opposites to the following:

B 1 absent ...*present*............   2 emigrant ....
    3 ascent ....   4 encourage ....
    5 interior....................   6 minimum ....
    7 pro-nuclear power ....   8 increase ....

3 By changing one of the following suffixes: -ful/-less   -ible/-less
Add the correct suffix to give words opposite in meaning to the following:

C 1 harmful . *harmless*.........   2 useful ....
    3 sensible....................   4 painless ....
    5 pitiless....................   6 careful ....

4 By providing a new word: amateur/professional   adult/child   rear/front
Complete the following by adding the opposite of the word in *italics*:

D 1 Sam was an *amateur* boxer while his brother was a ....
    2 Every *child* must be accompanied by an ....
    3 It could be safer in the *rear* of the train than in the ....

Nouns opposite in meaning

These nouns are words which are opposite in meaning. They are antonyms:

arrival/departure   danger/safety   question/answer

Write the opposites of the following (the first letters are given to help you find the word in the dictionary):

E   1 friend – en*emy* ....   2 entrance – ex ....

3 solid – li ....   4 age – yo ....

5 war – pe ....   6 landlord – te ....

7 valley – mo ....   8 death – bi ....

9 victory – de ....   10 weakness – st ....

Adjectives opposite in meaning

Write the opposites of the following adjectives:

F   1 common – ra*re* ....   2 modern – an ....

3 negative – po ....   4 permanent – te ....

5 full – va ....   6 angry – pl ....

7 rough – ca ....   8 senior – ju ....

Adverbs opposite in meaning

Write the opposites of the following adverbs:

G   1 late – ea*rly* ....   2 sometimes – ne ....

3 everywhere – no ....   4 well – ba ....

5 seldom – of ....   6 fast – sl ....

Verbs opposite in meaning

Write the opposite of the following verbs:

H   1 accept – re*ject* ....   2 throw – ca ....

3 release – ca ....   4 allow – fo ....

5 employ – di ....   6 teach – le ....

7 fill – em ....   8 play – wo ....

9 pull – pu ....   10 remember – fo ....

15

Synonyms or words similar in meaning

Synonyms have a similar meaning but no two words are exactly alike:

took – grabbed, grasped, seized, clutched, snatched
grabbed – take roughly; grasped – take firmly; seized – take forcibly; clutched – take eagerly; snatched – take very hastily.

Complete the following, adding the most suitable word for *took*:

A 1 Caryl **snatched** the chestnuts out of the burning cinders.

   2 The mountaineer .... his axe and began the climb.

   3 The monkey .... the lady's handbag, and chewed it.

   4 The drowning girl .... at the lifebelt they threw to her.

Here are a number of synonyms for *walked*:

limped, toddled, waddled, marched, paced, shuffled, prowled, dawdled

Complete the following, adding the most suitable word for *walked*:

B 1 The little baby **toddled** towards her proud mother.

   2 The injured footballer .... from the field.

   3 The soldiers .... in good order to their barracks.

   4 The thief .... round the jeweller's premises.

   5 The ducks .... to their pond.

   6 The old man .... to the door in his carpet slippers.

   7 The worried captain .... up and down the quarter-deck.

   8 The tired boy .... behind all the others.

Here are a number of words which all mean pointing towards a target:

pointed – levelled, aimed, directed, trained

Complete the following, adding the most suitable word for *pointed*:

C 1 The conductor **pointed** his baton in my direction.

   2 The knight .... his lance as he rode on to the field.

   3 The guns were .... on to the ship.

   4 The archer .... at the target.

   5 The police .... a searchlight on the building.

Synonyms – choosing the right word

Synonyms have nearly the same meaning. Although the difference may be small it is important to give the exact meaning intended.
Here are the synonyms of strike with their meanings:

tap – to strike lightly; rap – a slight knock, heavier than tap; slap – blow with the open hand; cuff – a box on the ear; knock – a blow producing a noise; punch – a blow with a closed fist; hit – a sharp blow that connects; smite – a very heavy blow.

Complete the following, selecting the most suitable synonym for *strike*:

D 1 Edwyn **tapped** .... the barometer to check the weather.

2 Botham .... a glorious six out of the ground.

3 The farmer should not have .... the boy although he was impudent.

4 The giant tried to .... off the head of the monster.

5 Nicola .... Irma across the face.

6 The beggar .... on the door and asked for shelter.

7 The teacher .... her ruler on the desk to get attention.

Many nouns have synonyms. Here are the synonyms of show with their meanings:

display – show to the best advantage; tableau – silent and motionless show; spectacle – lavish visual display; pageant – brilliant play illustrating a place's history; parade – march in procession; exhibition – public display.

Complete the following, selecting the most suitable synonym for *show*:

E 1 The fireworks provided a magnificent **spectacle** ......

2 The .... told the history of the ancient castle.

3 The pony won first prize at the horse ....

4 The crowd waited for the .... of the Boys' Brigade to pass.

5 An .... of French paintings was shown in the art gallery.

6 The children presented a .... of the nativity scene in the stable.

7 The club gave a wonderful gymnastic ....

Classification – one name for many things

All things on earth may be divided into two classes or groups:

1 *Animate* (living things) – creatures and plants.
2 *Inanimate* (non-living things) – things that are fixed, cannot eat, cannot move around from place to place.

Underline the animate (living things) in the following lists:

A 1 tiger, table, buffalo, cradle, camel, armchair
    2 lark, owl, canal, canary, bandage, wallet
    3 flea, moth, barometer, tea-caddy, locust, toaster
    4 hammer, plaice, kipper, picture, engine, cod

Every object or thing can be placed in a general class either because it resembles other things or because of its purpose or use.
General classes include: animals, birds, fishes, insects, reptiles, flowers, trees, liquids, jobs, buildings, vehicles, instruments, games, clothes, ships, utensils.
Write one name from the general classes listed above for each of the following groups:

B 1 perch, shrimp, sardine, sturgeon .. *fish* ....
    2 oak, lime, juniper, cedar ....
    3 saucepan, kettle, frying-pan, colander ....
    4 wine, water, petrol, paraffin ....
    5 butterfly, ichneumon, aphis, wasp ....
    6 skittles, darts, lacrosse, football ....
    7 church, school, town hall, castle ....
    8 stoat, puma, monkey, weasel ....
    9 barque, dhow, schooner, hydrofoil ....
   10 iguana, snake, puff-adder, salamander ....
   11 cowboy, tailor, warden, stoker ....
   12 veronica, nightshade, bluebell, primula ....
   13 socks, sweater, t-shirt, kaftan ....
   14 chaffinch, starling, hornbill, fieldfare ....
   15 telescope, barometer, speedometer, clock ....
   16 ambulance, locomotive, pram, mail-van ....

These are the names of the groups listed below. They are not in order:

headgear, food, weapons, receptacles, capitals, roads, tools, musical instruments, relations, minerals, residences, cereals, footwear, meats.

In the lists of words there is an outsider in each group.
Draw a line through the word that does not belong to the group.

C 1 turban, beret, cap, hat, ~~cheese~~   D 1 *headgear...*
   2 bungalow, street, house, palace, cottage   2 ....
   3 niece, uncle, mother, brother, doctor   3 ....
   4 pork, lamb, beef, cow, mutton   4 ....
   5 silver, lead, alcohol, bronze, iron   5 ....
   6 pistols, shotguns, rifles, fistulas, grenades   6 ....
   7 spear, spanner, hammer, screwdriver, chisel 7 ....
   8 Tokyo, Birmingham, London, Paris, Madrid   8 ....
   9 clogs, bolero, sandals, boots, shoes   9 ....
  10 avenue, square, lane, street, motorway   10 ....
  11 purse, wallet, belt, handbag, box   11 ....
  12 beer, bacon, sausage, toast, butter   12 ....
  13 rye, wheat, potatoes, barley, oats   13 ....
  14 trumpet, flute, violin, piano, radio   14 ....

D Write the correct name of each group on the line beside the list above.
Underline one word from each group in the brackets which belongs to the same classification as the first three words on the same line:

E 1 opal, ruby, sapphire   (silver, <u>emerald</u>, fossil)
   2 reporter, journalist, reviewer   (editor, adjutant, actor)
   3 dean, vicar, archbishop   (lawyer, curate, cathedral)
   4 shirt, jeans, trousers   (jersey, satin, woollens)
   5 recorder, clarinet, fife   (piccolo, register, buffoon)
   6 defeat, retreat, flight   (deadlock, overwhelm, rout)
   7 sin, misdemeanour, crime   (innocence, felony, faultless)
   8 nursery-man, planter, arborist   (small-holder, angler, tenant)
   9 marionette, doll, dummy   (monument, puppet, pedestal)
  10 surfboard, aquaplane, waterski   (parachute, safari, scull)
  11 gale, typhoon, hurricane   (zephyr, squall, breeze)
  12 pigmy, dwarf, midget   (colossus, ogre, mite)

Classification – group terms

Classification is the arrangement of objects into groups or sets.
The groups are formed according to the characteristics they have in common. We give a name (collective nouns) to these groups to make them easier to describe and better to understand. Most of the things we use daily, or talk about daily, are put into groups and named.
These are special group terms used for some animate (living) objects or people:

band, team, flock, litter, plague, school, swarm, coven, squad, squadron, kennel, stable

Fill the gaps with the correct group term:

A 1 *stable* ...... of horses   2 .... of locusts
   3 .... of pilots   4 .... of sheep
   5 .... of insects   6 .... of cubs
   7 .... of soldiers   8 .... of whales
   9 .... of footballers   10 .... of witches
  11 .... of musicians   12 .... of dogs

These are special group terms used for some inanimate (non-living) objects:

bale, pack, tuft, collection, clump, batch, forest, wisp, wad, file, sheaf, posy

Fill the gaps with the correct group term:

B 1 *collection* .. of pictures   2 .... of hay
   3 .... of bushes   4 .... of £5 notes
   5 .... of flowers   6 .... of grass
   7 .... of cotton   8 .... of trees
   9 .... of loaves   10 .... of cards
  11 .... of corn   12 .... of documents

Complete the following with the most suitable group term:

C 1 an army of *soldiers* ....   2 a stud of ....
   3 a crew of ....   4 a clutch of ....
   5 a menagerie of ....   6 a fleet of ....
   7 an orchestra of ....   8 a choir of ....

9 an exhibition of .... 10 a wardrobe of ....
11 an arcade of .... 12 a group of ....
13 a library of .... 14 an aviary of ....

These terms all apply to groups of people:

spectators, mob, congregation, audience, queue, community, gang, clan, club, crowd, team

Complete the following with the most suitable group term from the list above. One or two terms are suitable in more than one sentence. Try to use the most suitable, and, in any case, do not use the same term twice.

D 1 The Scots who belonged to the same ..clan...... wore the same tartan.
   2 The village hall served the whole ....
   3 The .... watched the exhibition of fireworks.
   4 The .... waited patiently for the next bus to arrive.
   5 The .... of thieves were caught when their car broke down.
   6 It is impossible to join the .... unless you are an angler.
   7 The .... were conspicuous in their red jerseys and white shorts.
   8 The vicar preached to the .... in the church.
   9 The .... looted the burnt-out shop.
   10 The orchestra played to the .... in the concert hall.
   11 A .... gathered in the park for the ceremony.

Can you find out the group terms used for the following?

E 1 badgers   ....   2 peacocks ....
   3 angels   ....   4 kittens   ....
   5 ants   ....   6 bells   ....

Similes and analogies

Similes compare things which are alike in some particular aspect although they may differ in other respects:

as swift as a deer   as white as a sheet   as cold as ice

Some similes are based on the distinctive qualities of animate (living) things:

agile monkey   blind bat   brave lion   cunning fox   sober judge
gentle dove   strong horse   fat pig   wise owl   mean miser

Complete the following, using the above list:

A 1 as fat as a .. pig ....   2 as mean as a ....

   3 as brave as a ....   4 as wise as an ....

   5 as gentle as a ....   6 as strong as a ....

   7 as sober as a ....   8 as agile as a ....

   9 as blind as a ....   10 as cunning as a ....

Some similes are based on the distinctive qualities of inanimate (non-living) things.
These are inanimate things with distinctive qualities:

doornail   peas   needle   pancake   barrel   fiddle   iron   lead   mustard   lightning

Complete the following, using the most suitable object from the above list:

B 1 as quick as . lightning ......   2 as fit as a ....

   3 as dead as a ....   4 as sharp as a ....

   5 as hard as ....   6 as like as two ....

   7 as keen as ....   8 as round as a ....

   9 as flat as a ....   10 as heavy as ....

Analogies compare things by using parallel cases.

west   flock   smell   feathers   school

Complete the following analogies from the above list:

C 1 *South* is to *north* as *east* is to . west ....

   2 *Shoal* is to *herring* as .... is to *whales*.

   3 *Sight* is to *eye* as .... is to *nose*.

   4 .... are to *bird* as *scales* are to *fish*.

   5 *Herd* is to *cattle* as .... is to *sheep*.

22

Gradation and association

Gradation indicates degrees of comparison:

Time (shortest first):   second   minute   hour   day   week   month
Feeling (lightest first):   touch   rap   knock   punch   batter

Place each of the following group of words in correct order – least first:

A 1 millimetre   kilometre   metre   centimetre   (measures)

millimetre   centimetre   metre   kilometre

2 Everest   Ben Nevis   Mont Blanc   Snowdon   Skiddaw   (mountains)

....

3 squirrel   deer   fox   mouse   stoat   (animals)

....

4 palace   cottage   hut   mansion   (homes)

....

5 shouted   whispered   roared   talked   (speech)

....

6 ran   marched   strolled   walked   (speed)

....

Association is the connection between related things or ideas:

Fruit: orange   apple   fig   melon   pear
Time: clock   watch   sundial   egg-timer

Underline the three words in the following groups which are associated with the word in *italics*:

B 1 *Tools:*   screwdriver   spanner   plastic   rifle   chisel

2 *Instruments:*   barometer   spade   kettle   anometer   tachograph

3 *Car:*   carburettor   rudder   radiator   gearbox   reservoir

4 *Ship:*   astronaut   chronometer   quadrant   prow   motorway

5 *Bicycle:*   anvil   chain   pedal   spinnaker   tandem

6 *Train:*   tender   bogie   rickshaw   hovercraft   buffer

★ Now test yourself in choosing words

Add prefixes to give words opposite in meaning to the following:

A 1 .... able   2 .... obey   3 .... accurate

   4 .... patient   5 .... regular   6 .... behave

Change the prefixes to give words opposite in meaning to the following:

B 1 export ....   2 include ....   3 inside ....

Add suffixes to give words opposite in meaning to the following:

C 1 fearful ....   2 useful ....   3 careful ....

   foreigner   adult   good   safety   beneficial   contract

Write the opposites of the following, choosing words from the above list:

D 1 harmful ....   2 expand ....

   3 native ....   4 danger ....

   5 evil ....   6 child ....

   cure   behaviour   conversation   love   necessary   wasteful

Write words similar in meaning to the following from the above list:

E 1 extravagant.................   2 affection ....

   3 essential ....   4 remedy ....

   5 talk ....   6 conduct ....

In the following lists draw a line through the word that is out of place:

F 1 chaffinch, sparrow, owl, frog, hawk   G 1 ....

   2 cod, plaice, ape, carp, mackerel   2 ....

   3 buttercup, cheese, snowdrop, lily, pansy   3 ....

   4 oak, flute, beech, willow, ash   4 ....

G Write the names of the groups listed above in the space provided above.

Write out the group terms used for the following:

H 1 .... of sheep   2 .... of horses

   3 .... of witches   4 .... of bells

   5 .... of teachers   6 .... of bees

Choosing the correct phrase – idioms

These words all mean coming 'to a conclusion' but can have special meanings:
  ended, finished, closed, concluded, completed, stopped

Complete the following with the most appropriate word from the above list:

A 1 The watch had .**stopped**........ at the time of the attack.

   2 The chairperson .... the meeting with a vote of thanks.

   3 The innings .... when the last man was caught.

   4 The boy .... his exam work on the stroke of time.

   5 Next week the serial in the magazine will be ....

   6 The workman .... painting the door.

Some words go together to make phrases known as idioms.
An idiom is a phrase approved by usage. These are idiomatic phrases:

  to take after   to take up   to take on
  to take over   to take down   to take off

Complete the following with the most appropriate word:

B 1 She took ..**up**..... tennis when she was only ten years old.

   2 The baby took .... her mother.

   3 The receptionist quickly took .... the message.

   4 The manager took .... the company and ran it himself.

   5 The plane took .... from the runway.

   6 The champion took .... all comers.

These are idiomatic phrases:

  (a) far and away; (b) once and for all; (c) to have cold feet;
  (d) to be all ears; (e) to bury the hatchet; (f) to give the game away.

Pair up the following with the most appropriate phrase from the list:

C 1 to be eager to listen ..**(d)**......   2 to let out a secret ....

   3 to be anxious ....   4 finally ....

   5 very much ....   6 to be friends again ....

Choosing the correct word – people and occupations

These are names given to occupations, trades, professions and jobs:

jockey   optician   detective   astronomer   architect   surgeon   mason

Complete the following definitions from the list above:

A 1 A .mason...... builds with stone.

2 A .... rides horses in races.

3 A .... investigates crimes.

4 An .... designs buildings.

5 An .... studies the stars and other heavenly bodies.

6 A .... is a doctor who performs operations.

7 An .... tests eyesight and sells spectacles.

These are occupations:

farmer   mechanic   vicar   referee   postman   musician   nurse   pilot
butcher   electrician

With which occupation listed above do you associate the following:

B 1 flute ..musician............   2 thermometer ....

3 plough ....   4 fuses and wires ....

5 mail ....   6 whistle ....

7 spanner ....   8 pulpit ....

9 altimeter .... 10 cleaver ....

These are names given to types of persons:

gossip   donor   addict   miser   optimist

Complete the following definitions from the list above:

C 1 A .miser..... is a person who hoards money.

2 A .... is a person who gives money or things to others.

3 A .... is a person who spreads idle talk about other people.

4 An .... is a person unable to free himself or herself from a habit.

5 An .... is a person who looks on the bright side.

Choosing the correct word – places and containers

Places which have special purposes:

gymnasium   brewery   nursery school   dispensary   aviary   stadium
dairy   laboratory   quarry   garage

Complete the following definitions from the list above:

D 1 Children are taught in a ..nursery school..............
   2 Beer is made or brewed in a ....
   3 Medicines are prepared in a ....
   4 Birds are kept in an ....
   5 Cars are kept and repaired in a ....
   6 Physical exercises take place in a ....
   7 Stone is dug out of the ground at a ....
   8 Sports are held within the arena of a ....
   9 Milk is made into butter and cheese in a ....
  10 Scientific experiments are conducted in a ....

Containers which are the receptacles for special articles are:

scabbard   wallet   hamper   bunker   caddy   creel   purse   wardrobe
pocket   holster   cistern   cabinet

With which container listed above do you associate the following?

E 1 porcelain ..cabinet..........   2 coins ....
   3 handkerchief ....   4 fish ....
   5 clothes ....   6 tea ....
   7 coal ....   8 sword ....
   9 water .... 10 £5 notes ....
  11 pistol .... 12 picnic food ....

Give the special names for the areas or pitches where the following are played:

F 1 bowls ....green/crown.....   2 golf (inland) ....
   3 boxing ....   4 golf (seaside) ....
   5 skating ....   6 tennis ....
   7 skittles ....   8 running ....

Choosing interesting words – sounds and words (inanimate)

Some words resemble the sounds associated with objects or actions (onomatopoeia). Their use adds to the meaning of the words.

Words used on their own with exclamation marks:

tick-tock! (ticking of a clock)   rat-tat! (knock)   ting-a-ling! (bicycle bell)
plop! plop! (water dripping)

Complete the following with words from the list above:

A 1 *Plop! plop!* ... The water dripped from the spout.
  2 .... Tim sounded his bicycle bell at the corner.
  3 .... The clock told us that time was passing.
  4 .... The knock on the door was heard again.

Words (like bang) which resemble sudden and violent noise:

blast (explosion)   pealing (bells)   screeching (brakes)   wailing (siren)
crackling (of wood)

Complete the following with words from the above list:

B 1 The *blast* ..... of the explosion could be heard in the quarry.
  2 The wedding was celebrated with the .... of bells.
  3 The .... of twigs underfoot could be heard in the wood.
  4 The car swerved off the road with the .... of brakes.
  5 The .... of the police car's siren stopped the traffic.

Quiet or persistent sounds:

chime (clock)   swish (dress)   clink (coin)   patter (rain)   splutter (engine)

Complete the following with words derived from those listed above:

C 1 There was the *clink* ..... of coins in the collector's box.
  2 She liked to hear the .... of her party dress as she danced.
  3 He listened happily to the .... of the clock.
  4 The .... of the rain on the window disturbed the baby.
  5 The engine .... once or twice and then failed.

Choosing interesting words – sounds and words (animate)

Words describing animal sounds often resemble the sound itself:

   an ape gibbers   a dog barks   a bear growls

Some words which imitate a sound are usually used on their own with exclamation marks:

   hee-haw! caw! baa! cluck! cock-a-doodle-doo! moo!

Complete the following with the appropriate word from the list above:

C 1 The hen goes .cluck.........   2 The cock goes...............

    3 The donkey goes ....   4 The sheep goes ....

    5 The rooks go ....   6 The cow goes ....

These words describe bird sounds:

   screeches coos gobbles sings crows quacks hoots cackles screams twitters

Complete the following with the appropriate word from the list above:

D 1 The owl ...hoots............   2 The parrot ....

    3 The sparrow ....   4 The lark ....

    5 The turkey ....   6 The dove ....

    7 The duck ....   8 The seagull ....

    9 The cock .... 10 The hen ....

These words describe animal sounds:

   brays roars lows grunts bellows hisses growls neighs bleats howls

Complete the following with the appropriate word from the list above:

E 1 The sheep .bleats...........   2 The snake ....

    3 The lion ....   4 The horse ....

    5 The bear ....   6 The donkey ....

    7 The bull ....   8 The cow ....

    9 The wolf.................. 10 The pig ....

These words describe insect sounds:

   buzzes hums chirps

Complete the following with the appropriate word from the list above:

F 1 The cricket ....   2 The bee ....   3 The fly ....

★ Now test yourself and check your rating

Write these words in alphabetical order:

A 1 ensign   padlock   temple   conqueror   ensnare

....

   2 inflame   rumour   infant   infinity   rummy

....

Underline the root parts of the following words:

B 1 television 2 century 3 pedal 4 November 5 predict 6 liberty

Here are six verbs: sang, listened, muttered, frowned, smiled, worked.
Complete the following with the most appropriate word from the above list:

C 1 She .... happily.   2 She .... gloomily.

   3 She .... inaudibly.   4 She .... attentively.

   5 She .... tunefully.   6 She .... vigorously.

Add prefixes to give words opposite in meaning to the following:

D 1 .... happy   2 .... obey   3 .... polite

   4 .... distinctly   5 .... fiction   6 .... possible

Write words with the correct suffix to give an opposite meaning to:

E 1 useful ....   2 painless ....   3 careful ....

Complete the following with the most suitable nouns:

F 1 a menagerie of ....   2 a fleet of ....

   3 a posy of ....   4 an aviary of ....

Complete the following with the name of the most suitable animal:

G 1 as brave as a ....   2 as cunning as a ....

   3 as blind as a ....   4 as fat as a ....

Complete the following with the most appropriate word:

H 1 The thieves broke .... the bank.

   2 We break .... for our holidays on Friday.

   3 The prisoner broke .... of jail.

Answers

Now test yourself (building a vocabulary) (page 13)
A 1 autogiro, Kalmuck, lumbago, monster, wampum.   2 plasticine, plateau, plonk, plough, plump.   3 concert, concrete, condemn, condor, convent.   4 dividend, Dixie, gadzooks, galipot, sanctuary.
B 1 li<u>b</u>erty, in<u>f</u>allible, <u>O</u>ctober, im<u>p</u>ort, na<u>v</u>igate.   2 <u>l</u>aboratory, <u>t</u>entacles, <u>u</u>nity, re<u>p</u>el, poli<u>t</u>ics.   3 <u>p</u>edestrian, <u>p</u>rimitive, <u>m</u>anual, <u>f</u>ortify, <u>r</u>otund.   4 re<u>v</u>oke, <u>d</u>ecimal, <u>c</u>reature, <u>a</u>queduct, re<u>v</u>olve.
C 1 <u>tract</u> = to draw;   2 <u>path</u> = feeling;   3 <u>ped</u> = foot;   4 <u>meter</u> = measure.
D 1 <u>pre</u> = before;   2 <u>trans</u> = across;   3 <u>inter</u> = between.
E 1 <u>-ful</u> = full of;   2 <u>-ant</u> = one who;   3 <u>-ess</u> = the female.

Now test yourself (choosing words) (page 24)
A 1 unable;   2 disobey;   3 inaccurate;   4 impatient;   5 irregular;   6 misbehave.
B 1 import;   2 exclude;   3 outside.
C 1 fearless;   2 useless;   3 careless.
D 1 harmless;   2 contract;   3 foreigner;   4 safety;   5 good;   6 adult.
E 1 wasteful;   2 love;   3 necessary;   4 cure;   5 conversation;   6 behaviour.
F 1 frog;   2 ape;   3 cheese;   4 flute.
G 1 fruits;   2 birds;   3 fish;   4 flowers;   5 animals;   6 trees.
H 1 flock;   2 stud/team;   3 coven;   4 peal or ring;   5 staff;   6 swarm/hive.

Now test yourself (page 30) (Check your rating.)

Count 5 points for the correct order in A 1 and A 2. No marks otherwise. For the rest count 5 points for each correct answer. You could score 170 for all correct answers.

A 1 conqueror, ensign, ensnare, padlock, temple;
   2 infant, infinity, inflame, rummy, rumour.
B 1 <u>tele</u>;   2 <u>cent</u>;   3 <u>ped</u>;   4 <u>Nov</u>;   5 <u>dict</u>;   6 <u>liber</u>.
C 1 smiled;   2 frowned;   3 muttered;   4 listened;   5 sang;   6 worked.
D 1 un-...   2 dis-...   3 im-...   4 in-...   5 non-...   6 im-...
E 1 useless;   2 painful;   3 careless.
F 1 animals;   2 ships/cars;   3 flowers;   4 birds.
G 1 lion;   2 fox;   3 bat;   4 pig.
H 1 into;   2 up;   3 out.

Rating Chart
Over 150:   Excellent.
130 to 150:   Very good indeed.
110 to 130:   Good.
 90 to 110:   Fair.
Below 90:   Check your mistakes. Try the exercises again.

This Headway edition first published 1991
by Hodder and Stoughton Educational,
a division of Hodder and Stoughton Ltd,
Mill Road, Dunton Green, Sevenoaks, Kent

British Library Cataloguing in Publication Data
Taylor, Boswell
　Test your child's good English.
　1. Grammar
　I. Title　II. Taylor, Boswell. *Test your child's grammar*　III. Series
　415

ISBN 0–340–54819–3

Copyright © 1983 Boswell Taylor

All rights reserved. No part of this publication may be reproduced or transmitted in any form or by any means, electronic or mechanical, including photocopy, recording, or any information storage and retrieval system, without permission in writing from Hodder and Stoughton Ltd.

Printed and bound in Great Britain by
Cambus Litho, East Kilbride